Trucks

by
Gail Saunders-Smith

Pebble Books

an imprint of Capstone Press

Pebble Books are published by Capstone Press
1710 Roe Crest Drive, North Mankato, Minnesota 56003
www.capstonepub.com

Books published by Capstone Press are manufactured with paper
containing at least 10 percent post-consumer waste.

Library of Congress Cataloging-in-Publication Data
Saunders-Smith, Gail.
Trucks / by Gail Saunders-Smith.
p. cm.
Summary: In simple text and photographs, describes a variety of trucks and what they do, including garbage trucks, cement mixers, snow plows, and mail trucks.
ISBN-13: 978-1-56065-496-4 (hardcover)
ISBN-10: 1-56065-496-1 (hardcover)
ISBN-13: 978-1-56065-967-9 (softcover pbk.)
ISBN-10: 1-56065-967-X (softcover pbk.)
1. Trucks—Juvenile literature. [1. Trucks.] I. Title.
TL230.15.S28 1997
629.224—DC21 97-23582
CIP
AC

Editorial Credits
Lois Wallentine, editor; Timothy Halldin and James Franklin, designer;
Michelle L. Norstad, photo researcher

Photo Credits
Unicorn Stock/H. H. Thomas, 6; Jeff Greenberg, 10; Aneal Vohra, 20
Valan Photos/John Schakel Jr., cover; A. B. Joyce, 1, 16; Brian Atkinson, 4;
B. N. Joyce, 8; J. A. Wilkinson, 12; Michael J. Johnson, 14
Waverly Traylor Photography, 18

Printed in the United States of America in North Mankato, Minnesota.
112012
006986R

Table of Contents

Little Rock
TRUCKING LTD.
N.B.

Trucks carry logs.

HEIL
91
476-0480
91
91
18

Trucks haul garbage.

MILK
MMB
MILK
TPG 553X

Trucks hold milk.

JOEL
TANIS
& SONS

Trucks mix concrete.

445-3479
646-6424

Trucks dump rocks.

GMC
EM1 773

Trucks plow snow.

CRANVEL

Trucks lift people.

Trucks tow cars.

3195744
264

Trucks bring mail.

Words to Know

concrete—a building material made from cement, sand, gravel, and water

dump—to empty

garbage—things people throw out

haul—to carry

plow—to remove or push aside

tow—to drag behind

truck—a large motor vehicle

Read More

Johansen, Heidi Leigh. *My Book of Trucks.* Getting to Know My World. New York: PowerKids Press, 2005.

Schaefer, Lola M. *Tow Trucks.* The Transportation Library. Mankato, Minn.: Bridgestone Books, 2000.

Williams, Linda D. *Earthmovers.* Mighty Machines. Mankato, Minn.: Capstone Press, 2005.

Internet Sites

FactHound offers a safe, fun way to find Internet sites related to this book. All of the sites on FactHound have been researched by our staff.

Here's how:

1. Visit *www.facthound.com*
2. Type in this special code **1560654961** for age-appropriate sites. Or enter a search word related to this book for a more general search.
3. Click on the **Fetch It** button.

FactHound will fetch the best sites for you!

Note to Parents and Teachers

This book describes and illustrates a variety of trucks and what they do. Each sentence includes a new verb and an object that helps identify the type of truck. The photographs clearly illustrate the text and support the child in making meaning from the words. Children may need assistance in using the Table of Contents, Words to Know, Read More, Internet Sites, and Index/Word List sections of the book.

Index/Word List

Word Count: 27
Early-Intervention Level: 6